Creating the 100mph Hitter

by Mike Ryan

Contents

Acknowledgements

Without these people, this system is NOT possible.

I want to thank my kids—Jimmy, Maggie, and Jack—for the all the time they have given up to allow me to help others chase their dreams and accomplish their goals.

— My parents, Pat and Johanna Ryan, who instilled in me hard work and leadership and always supported me and my love for baseball.

— Steve Vandenbranden, who has coached at Fastball USA for more than ten years
and has helped mold the system that Fastball USA and Explosive Hitting is today.

— All of my students over the years that have dedicated themselves and made sacrifices to improve.

— Ron Wolforth of the Texas Baseball Ranch. He is a great friend and mentor, and I appreciate his guidance, friendship, and his never-ending passion to improve as a coach.

— My son Jack Ryan for all the time on demonstrations he has given us for this book, our hitting videos, and the many camps we do.

— Finally, and especially, my wife and best friend, Shelly Ryan, who has sacrificed time and supported my passion for baseball and the mission to help players improve from all over the world. Without you, none of this is possible.

Be Uncommon!

Mike Ryan, Fastball USA

Foreword

by Ron Wolforth

I have known Mike Ryan and his family for more than ten years now, and for eight of those years I have conducted two pitching clinics per year at their facility. Mike, Shelly, Steve, Paddy, and the entire Fastball family are a truly remarkable team. They have taken Ranch concepts and applied them in their own unique way.

They are not only caring, compassionate teachers and innovators, but more importantly, they are simply wonderful, honest, sincere people. I consider Fastball USA to be an extension of me and our Texas Baseball Ranch. I have a special place in my heart for the Ryans and all the athletes that train at Fastball. I truly look forward to my visits every year and to see how Mike has applied my pitching concepts to his passion, which is hitting.

If you get the opportunity to train with Mike and Steve, I could no more highly recommend it.

Ron Wolforth
Texas Baseball Ranch

Chapter One – Introducing Coach Mike Ryan

Hi, I'm Coach Mike Ryan, and in this book I will outline for you exactly how to become a 100mph hitter and why working towards the 100mph mark is huge when it comes to developing into a great hitter.

100mph hitter? Sound like an odd concept? The fact is if you're going to be able to hit home runs, you have to have a swing that creates 100mph ball exit speed.

I'm going to show you exactly why these training concepts will be the key to hitting more home runs and how improving ball exit speed will improve your hitting power forever.

First, let me tell you about myself.

I am the owner and director of baseball training of Fastball USA, which is an elite baseball academy near Chicago, Illinois. Players from all over the United States come to Fastball USA to train. I have also spent the past 15 years as an associate scout with the Seattle Mariners organization.

My specialty is baseball power development and very specifically hitting and throwing power. I have been coaching hitters professionally for the past 17 years.

MIKE RYAN

It's important for you to understand that I was not a doctor of baseball power when I started out, and it took time and a lot of years to figure this thing out.

The road to understanding baseball power development was a slow and gradual process. From 1997 to 2004, not even one of my students was drafted, and not a single student hit or threw a baseball 90mph.

The thing that bothered me most as coach and as a scout was really simple. What I and other people are looking for, as a scout is not what I was developing as a baseball instructor. It is also NOT what most instructors are emphasizing.

Scouts are looking for things that most people believe can't even be taught. Most believe you either have it or you don't have it. The "it" I am referring to is baseball power.

I refer to the big three. The greatest players in the world can do the following:

1.   Hit Harder
2.   Run Faster
3.   Throw Harder

Generally, if you can do two of those three things better than everyone else in your age group, you're really going to stand out. If you can do all three, you have a very special opportunity.

The general rule of thumb is that you can't teach power.

CREATING THE 100MPH HITTER

Scouts believe that power is something you have and not something that can be developed. The result is that the players that are most likely to be drafted into professional baseball are those who can hit the hardest, run the fastest, and throw faster than everyone else.

You can have a great eye at the plate, but if you can't drive the baseball, then scouts will pass you up. Hitting power is very rare and really stands out.

I am here to tell you that if you want to stand out, you need to improve hitting power.

Once I changed my emphasis as a coach and an instructor to developing baseball power, my world has changed, which has led to writing this book.

What results?

Remember, during my first eight years of training baseball players, I had no players drafted and no players touch 90mph of throwing or hitting speed.

Since 2005 that has all changed. I have had eight of my students drafted into professional baseball, and more than 100 of my students have either thrown or hit a baseball 90mph or more.

Even more impressive, I have had 11 players now become 100mph athletes by either throwing or hitting a baseball 100mph or more.
Yes—I said 100mph. Yes—100mph does transfer to power in a game.

In addition to the drafted players, I now have students all over the country playing college baseball including top Division I programs.

Most would not have attained the level they are playing at without the addition of baseball power and in most cases baseball hitting power.

The change? In my first few years of instructing, I pretty much taught what I was taught as a player. It's a natural course for a coach to simply repeat and teach whatever he was taught as a player.

The best thing I ever did was to begin questioning everything I ever did as a coach and began researching and experimenting with improved methods. I took being a paid instructor very seriously, which led me to studying concepts in other sports and talented baseball people around the country.

The main difference was a change in philosophy. The philosophy slowly became that speed and power must come first, while we work on precision in the process.

The change in philosophy was to stop focusing on looking pretty and start focusing on results.

My program is focused on being results-oriented as opposed to just looking good or just focusing on the process without paying attention to the results.

Early in my days as an instructor, I focused on mechanics to a point where hitters became mechanical.

CREATING THE 100MPH HITTER

I focused on getting hitters to look better, but looking better does not always equal results.

I focused on positions of hitting to a point where we would break hitting down into steps. Maybe you have seen it done or have experienced it yourself. For example, step 1, stride and load; step 2, pivot your back foot; step 3, swing the bat.

I now focus on the movement of hitters because hitting is a movement by definition. Hitting is not a position. If you move well and move efficiently and move quickly, you can become a much more powerful hitter.

I now focus on getting hitters to be athletic or being an athlete with a bat in your hand.

I now focus on objectively measuring everything we do. By objectively measuring progress, it gives my students facts about development as opposed to my opinion.

Lastly and really simply: in my opinion hitting development is NOT simply looking better or looking how some coach wants you to look.

Hitting development is about undisputed objectively measured results. It's about fact, not opinion.

Why is this so important?

Every hitting coach in the world has his own view of what good mechanics are and what a great hitter should look like. The problem is that you can't force everyone to look exactly alike.

Hitting styles are dangerous because one hitting method can't possibly work for everyone.

With my system of developing 100mph hitters, we let the facts determine if we are heading in the right direction.

Anything you measure, you can improve.

Chapter Two - Why 100mph?

What's the big deal about hitting a ball 100mph? This is not just some random number I picked. Here is why you need to train towards 100mph ball exit speeds. To be clear—ball exit speed means how fast the ball comes off your bat.

Studies have shown that in order to hit a home run, a ball needs to travel off the bat at a minimum of 90 miles per hour. Let's say a short homerun is 300 feet, which is about right for the shortest distances in ballparks. For the ball to go that far, it's going to have to be traveling a minimum of 90 miles per hour. This number is referred to as ball exit speed.

Advanced technology used by Major League Baseball is showing us that a great majority of home runs are hit right around 100mph off the bat. Let's look at one of the best hitters in the game, Mike Trout of the Los Angeles Angels. Mike hit 36 homeruns in 2014 at an average speed of 103 miles per hour. Another example—the two fastest ball exit speeds in 2014 belonged to David Ortiz of the Boston Red Sox and Giancarlo Stanton of the Miami Marlins, each of whom hit homeruns at 119.9 miles per hour. Those were the hardest-hit balls of the entire 2014 season.

What do these numbers mean? They mean that if you want to be a power hitter, you're going to have to hit the ball at a minimum of 90mph. If you want greater ball exit speed, then you're going to need to pay close attention to how fast the ball jumps off your bat.

Assuming that that the ball has good trajectory, the ball exit speed will determine how far the ball will travel. If you're going to hit the ball further and hit more homeruns, then the key is training yourself to become a 100mph hitter.

The second thing is that all the scouts out there who are scouting high school and college players are looking for guy who can hit the ball harder and farther then everybody else. Scouts want to see hitters that can hit the ball hard, even when they're making outs. So if I'm a young hitter going to a showcase, and I have a wooden bat in my hand and I'm just taking batting practice in front of 30 scouts, I need to be able to stand out in some way. And the only way to stand out in a situation with a wood bat in my hand in front of those 30 scouts is to hit the ball harder and/or farther than everybody else.

Showcases are now tracking ball exit speed. If you're a high school student looking to get noticed by top colleges, it would help to improve ball exit speed. The top showcase events in the country are including ball exit speed as a number that college coaches can now look at when recruiting. Many of my own students dominate in ball exit speed testing. It is common that a Fastball USA student is at the top in ball exit speed rankings.

The other thing all players attending showcases need to consider is how to get recruited. In many showcase events, you take batting practice on a field, which leaves your hitting open to a coach's opinion. If you're hitting the ball further than everyone else, it is an obvious way to stand out in batting practice. Otherwise, they can only form an opinion about what your swing looks like, which is different for every coach and scout. Power is something that most feel can't be taught. Power is a difference maker and a separator.

Again, you're looking at homerun distances of at least 300 feet, so if you leave the showcase that day and you're one of the few guys who have hit the ball over the fence or driven the ball to the fence over and over again, you're going to stand out above the other hitters at the showcase.

Remember, scouts are looking for players who have power. Most scouts feel that power cannot be taught. They believe that power in a hitter is a special quality. Obviously, I disagree that it can't be taught, but it is something special. If you want to stand out and increase your chances of getting a look from pro scouts or top colleges, then you need to start working on your power right now. Improving power is very likely if you are focusing on improving ball exit speed and you continue to work towards one day becoming a 100mph hitter. The harder you hit the ball, the farther it's going to travel, and the more you'll stand out as a prospect to a pro organization.

Words from a Valued Client

My son Max Jr. had just received an invitation to USA Baseball's 12U National Open. After learning we had approximately three months to prepare, I reached out to our good friend Ron Wolforth at Texas Baseball Ranch. I asked him who I could take Max to for help with his swing, and he said there's one guy I trust to help develop power and explosiveness in Max. The one thing that stayed with me is that Ron said Mike Ryan's Fastball USA is for hitting what the Texas Baseball Ranch is for pitching.

Upon our arrival at Fastball USA, Mike Ryan pulled out the radar and measured Max's swing with a drop 10 / 70 mph, drop 5 / 65 mph and a wood bat drop 3 / 63 mph. After three days of working with Mike, my son's radar readings were drop 10 / 74 mph, drop 5 / 71 mph and wood bat drop 3 / 67 mph. He gained an average of 4 mph of batted ball exit speed on all three bats.

While at USA Baseball's 12U National Open, my son went 9 for 14 with 2 home runs and 7 RBIs.

We have continued to follow Mike Ryan's Fastball USA program, and one year later, these are my son's radar readings: drop 10 / 83 mph, drop 5 / 78 mph and wood bat drop 3 / 75 mph. On average, we have gained 10 to 12 mph in one year.

I highly recommend Fastball USA for any parent that wants to help give his or her son or daughter an advantage over their competition.

The smile says it all.

Max Soliz

Chapter Three - The 100mph Mindset

Is hitting the ball 100mph all about hitting homeruns? No way. Scouts are going to be looking at how hard you hit the ball anywhere on the field and in all situations. Part of hitting the ball harder is improving your percentage and the likelihood that you'll get on base.

For example, if I hit a ground ball five feet to the left of the shortstop and it leaves my bat at 80 miles an hour, then the shortstop has a little more time to get there, cut the ball off, and throw me out at first base. But if I hit the ball and the ball exit speed is 95 to 100 miles an hour, then the fielder has a lot less reaction time and that ball may just get through the infield for a base hit. So even on that specific swing, I may not hit the ball with the right trajectory for a homerun, but because I hit it so much harder, I have a much better chance of getting on base.

If you're going to be a hitter who can drive the baseball, you have to have a different mindset. My best students don't focus on batting average. My best students simply focus on hitting the ball harder.

Instead, I strongly suggest you focus on your percentage of hard-hit balls. How often you hit the ball hard is far more important than your batting average. I urge you to understand you can only control the things you can control. You can't control whether the other team catches the ball and gets you out. You can control your percentage of hard-hit balls.

For example, I can go 0-for-4 but hit all four balls hard. I may not have gotten a hit that day, but I hit the ball hard. On the other hand, I could get four bloop singles and be 4-for-4. But just because I'm batting 1.000 doesn't mean I'm hitting the ball well. At our academy, we get our guys focused on the percentage of hard-hit balls because ultimately that's what's going to build a better hitter.

Some people will argue with that and say, "Well, the guy who went 4-for-4 got on base and the other guy didn't." But what most people don't realize is that the guy with the bloop hits is probably already in a slump— he just got lucky at the plate. He got four balls to fall in for hits, but he's not hitting the ball hard, which gives him a much smaller chance overall of getting on base.

The big thing that happens here is that people think they're having success. You've just had a four-hit game, and you're down at the Dairy Queen celebrating with the team. But this is a short-term mindset. The reality is that you're already one step into a slump—you just don't realize it.

Now let's look at our other guy. He went 0 for 3, but he hit the ball hard every time. He's probably upset with his performance because he did not get a hit or reach base. The reality is that you need to have the 100mph hitter mindset: hitting the ball hard—and that's all you can control. You can only control whether you hit the ball hard, not if the other team caught the ball. I have seen hitters beat themselves up for not getting hits, even when they are hitting well. This is a mindset issue.

If you don't master this concept, you will always struggle mentally because you have a confused outlook.

If you start to look at it this way, it brings a completely different mindset and a completely different expectation. Great hitters master this mindset and understand that luck does not determine their fate.

At the end of the day, simply pay attention to how often you hit the ball hard in a game and in batting practice. Forget the batting average statistic. Become obsessed with following your percentage of hard-hit balls.

Chapter Four -
The Nine Keys to Training the 100mph Hitter

Now that we know why it's important to be a 100mph hitter, we need to talk about how. I have nine specific training keys that are essential to being able to accomplish this feat. We've developed these nine concepts over the past ten years, and they've led to the great success with players' results that we talked about earlier.

1. Master the Mission

The first, and most important, key to training is to master the mission, which means have a very clear intent. The intent or mission should be to hit the ball hard. What's different about our best students is that they all have the mission or obsession to hit the ball hard and to hit the ball far.

The mission is to hit the ball hard, period. The secondary mission is to have great ball flight or trajectory. Without focusing on this mission or having the intent to hit the ball hard, it makes it difficult to become a powerful hitter. I am telling you that the number-one secret to becoming a 100mph hitter is to have the intent or goal of hitting the ball as hard as possible.

There are two questions you should ask yourself after every single practice swing:

#1 Did I hit the ball hard?

If you can't answer yes, then you have no other question to ask. Return to the number-one goal and do whatever possible to accomplish this goal.

#2 If you hit the ball hard, then you only have one other question:

Did the ball have good flight?

The reality is that if you're going to hit the ball with home run power, you have to create home run trajectory.

I find that very few players actually really work on creating good ball flight. The definition of good ball flight in my world is somewhere between a line drive and airplane flight. Airplane flight is simply how a plane takes off rising. We want to avoid hitting balls into the ground and we want to avoid space shuttle flight, which is straight up.

Either way, I think a big mistake is that most hitters have been coached to become afraid of hitting the ball in the air. The reality is that if you hit the ball harder, then the ball in the air is hit further. The key to avoiding dreaded fly ball outs is actually hitting the ball harder.

You need to be obsessed with these two areas:

    A. Hitting the ball hard

B. Hitting the ball with good flight

The reason intent is so important is something I learned that I refer to as the Bernstein Principle. Nikolai Bernstein was a Russian neurophysiologist, meaning he worked with how the body learns motor skills. He was a specialist in biomechanics. He is considered to be the father of biomechanics.

What I discovered through studying Bernstein makes a lot of sense. He said, "The body will organize itself based on the ultimate goal of the activity." What he's saying, in baseball terms, is that your goal will strongly reflect or impact your mechanics. So, what your goal is will strongly influence how you're going to swing.

My life as an instructor changed when I began to understand this concept. Too many people spend too much time on how to swing, without considering how the goal itself will alter or determine how someone will swing. At the end of the day, you learn how to hit based on your goal, not based on just trying to look good while hitting.

Here's an example. Imagine a hitter who goes up to the plate trying to hit the ball as hard and as far as he can. Then compare him to another hitter who goes up to the plate just trying to make contact. Picture those two swings—can you imagine how the technique would change? One hitter, all he's trying to do is just hit the ball. The other hitter is trying to hit the ball 500 feet. That's what Bernstein is talking about—the body will organize itself based on the goal.

This is a powerful lesson and the Bernstein principle

is where everything begins in my training at Fastball USA. Your mechanics arrive based on your goal.

For most players and coaches today, they actually emphasize the opposite, and they focus on the process and hope the result happens.

No matter what you learn in this book, none of it matters unless you have a very clear intent, which is the mission to hit the ball hard with good ball flight.

2. Mindset of the 100mph Hitter

The second training key, once you have clear intent, is all about mindset. There are several components to having the right mindset, and the most important is aggressiveness. I know that's easier said than done. After all, many coaches think that a player is either aggressive or he's not. I don't believe that. I think that aggressiveness is developed by your environment.

A player with an aggressive mindset is not afraid to fail. So that's the next component: no fear of failure. Great athletes—and it doesn't matter what sport they play, whether it's baseball, basketball, football, or any other sport—are super-aggressive and aren't afraid to screw up. They're not afraid to fail. I like to tell our students that they cannot be afraid to look bad. Pete Rose once said that the three keys to good hitting are really simple. Number one, he said, was to be aggressive. Number two was to be even more aggressive. And number three was to never be satisfied. Obviously, Pete Rose was a great hitter, so I think we should listen to what he's got to say about hitting. It makes a lot of sense to me.

CREATING THE 100MPH HITTER

As a final word about mindset and aggressiveness, I want to give you an example. In my world, I think aggressiveness is like fire. You can either throw water on that fire, or you can throw fuel on the fire. The people around you are constantly either throwing water or throwing fuel on the fire. Let's look at a kid who comes up to the plate and swings aggressively at a pitch up around his eyes and misses. Obviously, he's being aggressive, but he swung at a bad pitch. So his coach or his mom or his dad is yelling at him, "What'd you swing at that one for?" And that's a problem. The kid was aggressive, he made a mistake, and now he's being yelled at for making that mistake. So his coaches and his parents are throwing water on the fire. And what happens almost every time in baseball is this—the next pitch is right down the middle, but the kid doesn't swing. Why doesn't he swing? Because he's now afraid of making a mistake and getting yelled at some more.

As coaches, as parents, and even as players and teammates, we need to create an environment where aggressiveness is encouraged and rewarded, an environment where people are not afraid to fail. They're actually encouraged to fail. Because failure is the first step in becoming more successful. And for us, that is huge.

Babe Ruth once said, "Never let the fear of striking out get in your way." That's a great quote. Somebody asked Mickey Mantle once if he ever tried to go to the plate hitting a homerun, and he answered, "Sure. Every time I went to the plate I tried to hit a homerun." I love both of those quotes, and I keep reinforcing those concepts with our athletes.

3. Measure the Mission

The third key to developing the 100mph hitter is measurement. Anything that can be measured can be improved. When we measure our progress, and by that I mean look at our progress objectively, we get objective feedback on how we're doing. The last thing you want is subjective feedback. Subjective feedback is simply some coach's opinion. In my world, opinion gets in the way because opinion is not about results. If you want to become a better hitter, if you want to hit the ball harder that you do today, you have to start measuring how hard you're hitting the ball.

There are several ways we take objective measurements. The number one measurement we use is ball exit speed. We set up 10 to 15 feet behind the batter with a radar gun while he's doing his batting tee work, and while he's hitting off the tee, he will get radar feedback on exactly how hard he's actually hitting the ball.

Most people, when they do batting tee work, they're just practicing their swing. That gets really boring, really fast. At our academy, what we do is actually measure how fast the ball is coming off the tee. And we don't just measure it; we also record it. The student will write down every number he gets. So, in terms of being objective, we're actually measuring our mission, which is how hard the ball was hit.

Now, going back to the second part of our mission—

did the ball have good flight?—we also have our students diagram where every ball is hit. So if the ball is hit into the ground, hit on a line drive, hit with airplane flight, hit to left, hit to right, hit dead center … the athlete records all of that. We're always hitting at targets and the hitters are always diagramming in a notebook where the ball is going. That way, when he's done, he has created more awareness of how he's actually doing. He's measuring how hard he hit the ball, and he's measuring and recording where the ball actually went.

Those are our top two measurements, but we measure other things as well that are very important when it comes to hitting harder with better ball flight.

We also measure the speed of the bat, so we have a bat speed radar that measures how fast the hitter can swing. Bat speed will help improve exit speed. In fact, the faster you swing is step 1 in creating more ball exit speed and distance.

Bat speed is very important, but clearly how fast the ball jumps off your bat is more important than bat speed. Bat speed really is measuring effort or energy put into the swing. The exit speed is the actual result. It is possible to have a swing with 100mph bat speed that only creates 75mph of ball exit speed. It's important to understand this concept. Bat speed will produce more exit speed when you square up the ball perfectly. Bat speed does us no good if we can't consistently hit the ball with precision.

The most important number is how hard the ball is hit.

In order to hit harder, you do need to create more bat speed. At Fastball USA, we measure both bat speed and ball exit speed, knowing that the ultimate goal is to improve the ball exit speed and ball flight.

It is common that our better hitters have ball exit speeds up to 8mph higher than their bat speed. This is a sign of a mechanically efficient hitter. If you can hit the ball harder than how fast you swing, it shows us that you are maximizing your effort. If your bat speed is equal to your exit speed, or your exit speed is slower that bat speed, then this shows us we can improve the efficiency of swing technique.

At the end of the day, my top three measurements that I want my students recording are bat speed, ball exit speed, and ball flight.

Now, for those who don't have equipment like radar guns, you can certainly at the very least record in your notebook where you're hitting the ball. The other way to objectively measure your progress is simply to measure the distance that you're hitting the ball. You can do this with a tee or with softball or batting practice. For example, if you're hitting on a field with a fence, you know how far it is to the fence. You could simply measure how far every ball is going not only on a fly, but on a ground ball as well. Measure how far it's going along with diagramming where you're hitting the ball, and that's going to create awareness and feedback on your progress as a hitter.

We have an old saying: "If you want to hit the ball harder, you have to practice hitting the ball harder," and that is absolutely true. If you want to swing faster, you have to practice swinging faster. And these measurements and objective feedback that you're getting will allow you to evaluate how you're doing. It's very important that you record it because it starts to give you goals going forward. For example, if I hit the ball 80 miles an hour today, and my average is 78, then the next time I'm out there, I have a specific goal: I'm going to try to beat 80 miles an hour. This is what we call the "video game" aspect of baseball training. And it creates a lot more awareness and a lot more fun in the process.

4. Slight edge

The idea of having a slight edge is a very simple one. Most people, when they're trying to improve on something, want to see all the improvement at once. They're always in a hurry. With the notion of the slight edge, we look for slight improvement over a long period of time.

Let's say, for example, that you wanted to gain 12 miles an hour of ball exit speed over the next year. How I look at slight edge here would be really simple. All you need to do is gain one mile an hour over the next month. I always ask my students, "Do you think it's possible for you to gain one mile an hour in the next 30 days?" And of course it's possible! But it's a completely different way of looking at it. The power of the slight edge is that I know I can gain one mile an hour over the next 30 days. I know I can create, say, five more feet of distance on my hits in the next 30 days. So the real secret to making big improvements is

23

not trying to gain 12 miles an hour in 10 weeks. The secret is to continually get better every day.

I always tell our students that they need to challenge themselves slightly beyond their current capability. Slightly beyond is very important. If it's too overwhelming, it's easy to give up and quit. But if you're not challenging yourself enough, you're not going to get better. Always challenge yourself slightly beyond where you're at, and that's where slight edge comes into play. I always tell our students to create goals—both short-term goals and long-term goals. So, a short-term goal might be to gain one mile an hour over the next 30 days, and a long-term goal might to be gain 12 miles an hour over the next year. But let's just take it 30 days at a time, and then let's see what happens over a year's time. What you start to find out is that in one, two, three years, it's very realistic that you can gain 10, 20, even 30 miles an hour if you have that mindset and that approach.

Most people, when faced with long-term goals, give up easily because they get frustrated. That's what happens for people who don't follow the slight edge concept. I would compare it to people who have trouble losing weight. We tend to give up easily if our mindset is, "I'm going to lose 30 pounds." But if the mindset is, for instance, "I'm going to lose one pound a week for the next 30 weeks," then that's very attainable. You can accomplish that! The slight edge concept works not just in baseball, but in just about anything in which you're trying to achieve a goal or make some progress.

5. Adapt and adjust

We've all heard this one: "Doing the same thing over and over again and expecting different results is the definition of insanity." That's why we need to adapt and adjust, and this is closely intertwined with our idea of intent and mission. If you're expecting a different result, you're going to have to stop doing the same thing over and over. What I tell all our students is that, as great players, they need to pay attention to the results and then they adapt and adjust from there. And this is why measuring is so important. If you're measuring everything you do—write it down, record it, document it—then you become more aware. And when you become more aware, you're more likely to make an adjustment. It's impossible to adjust if you don't know what you're adjusting from. You can't adjust to something if you don't know where you're at right now.

For example, let's say I'm a hitter and I'm trying to hit a line drive to the back of the batting cage. If I have a target set up right back at the batting cage, and I'm trying to hit a line drive right at it, but I keep missing my target low over and over, then I need to make an adjustment. Most hitters will not make the adjustment because they don't pay attention. The simple adjustment is instead of aiming for that target and continuing to miss low, I should be aiming higher than the target. I should be aiming up in order to hit that line drive. The same would hold true for a hitter who hits pop up after pop up, just one after another. If the hitter is trying to hit a line drive, he needs to adapt and adjust and try to hit the ball slightly down in order to hit his line drive.

Those are just a couple of examples of adjusting, and they both relate to our initial question—What is your goal? What is your intent? If your intent is to hit a hard line drive, or hit the ball as hard and as far as you can, and you're not succeeding, well, join the club. That's just going to happen. But once you see your result, you need to learn how to adapt and adjust your goal in order to create the result that you want. What I find is that the greatest hitters I've ever worked with are outstanding at making adjustments. And that's not just hitters, that's athletes in general. Great athletes are great at making adjustments.

Another way to look at the concept of adapt and adjust is that athletes are self-coaching, they're self-adjusting. Great athletes coach themselves. So, when I'm in our training center and I'm working with our athletes, I'm actually coaching them on how to coach themselves. I'm not the guy who needs to be their savior. They need to be on the field, ready to make adjustments at any point in time. So, if a hitter goes up there and he's 0-for-4 and he's hit four ground balls today, then he needs to be able to self-coach and self-adjust.

If a hitter is not practicing making adjustments in practice or when he's hitting on his own, then he's not going to be able to make adjustments in a game. You have to start by practicing making adjustments. My advice to parents is this—don't be so quick to make adjustments for your young athlete. Allow him during practice to struggle and fail, and then see if he can make his own adjustments and get out of it. You can guide him toward the adjustment, but don't always give away the answer. If we're spoon-feeding the answers to the kids, if we're always holding their hands, they're not going to become good at making adjustments.

6. Imitation

Think for a minute about a time not that long ago when we didn't have all this technology, didn't have access to video analysis, didn't have the internet where we could look up anything and anybody. How did the great hitters or the great athletes become great?

I would say that the number one way that hitters achieved greatness was through imitation. They watched other people do what they wanted to do, and then they would do it the same way. You always hear people tell the stories about how, when they were growing up, they followed a friend in the neighborhood or they did the same thing as their older brother. Or maybe they flipped on the television and watched their favorite hitter and then they would go outside and imitate that guy. Greatness can be achieved through imitation probably quicker than through any other method.

This is very powerful. When you imitate somebody doing something, you are far more likely to learn it quickly. So who do we encourage our kids to imitate? We want to imitate great hitters. Now, we can use the internet because there's so much video out there of baseball players, and specifically hitters, that we can actually watch them and study them and then go out on the field and imitate them. Imitation is much more powerful than somebody trying to talk you through what you should do.

At our training center, I sometimes take students and ask them to watch our best hitters, maybe pick out one thing, and just watch that really good hitter hit. And then I will say, "OK, let's go hit now. Let's go imitate what we saw." Imitating the good hitter becomes a drill, but they learn so much faster using that method than somebody trying to talk them through the process.

It's really that simple—if you want to become a great hitter, then you have to imitate great hitters. So you have to watch closely. My big piece of advice is that you need to watch the small things. I would watch pieces of movements, more than anything. Instead of watching the whole movement, I would just watch pieces. Focus on those small pieces and then right away go and try to imitate what you've been watching.

We've had players come through our academy who go on to college. Their college coach says something like, "Hey, your swing looks a lot like Bryce Harper's." And the kid would think, "Hey, thanks, what a great compliment." Then the coach says, "Well, you're not Bryce Harper." See, to me, that thought process is just ridiculous. If I'm trying to become a great hitter, I want to look like a great hitter. Why would I imitate anybody who's less than a great hitter? But that's the mindset of coaches throughout the country today—Bryce Harper is who he is because he's a freak of nature, not because of what he's doing. And coaches downplay how powerful our kids are today and some of the things they can do. They just assume that you are not a freak, therefore you can't hit like that.

So, at Fastball USA, I allow our players to imitate big

league hitters and to virtually generate their own style of hitting. We allow them to really study hitters and then implement what they've learned into their practice. This becomes a very powerful learning tool for them.

7. The 10,000-Hour Rule

At Fastball USA, we believe in the 10,000-Hour Rule. The 10,000-Hour Rule is based on a study stating that it takes 10,000 hours of deliberate practice to become truly elite in any field or any sport. Ten thousand hours. Now, we've seen this in action, and we believe it— when you work harder than everybody else, you get better. Especially when you work with specific intent and deliberate practice.

The alternative to the 10,000-Hour Rule is what people call the prodigy theory, or some people call it the "freak" theory. The prodigy theory believes that somebody was just simply born to do something well. Again, a lot of people say this about Bryce Harper—he is the way he is, that is, he's a great player, because he's a freak. He was born a freak and that's why he's good. But when you really look into Bryce Harper's background, you'll start to realize that when he was 10 and 11 years old, he was practicing four or five hours a day, taking millions and millions of swings in order to get better. He never took hitting lessons. His whole intent was to hit the ball harder and farther than everybody else, and he simply worked longer and harder. Most people don't even want to believe in the 10,000-Hour Rule because they want to take shortcuts. They want to go for a private lesson but then not practice any other time and just rely on the lesson.

The reality is, how hard you work, how many hours you put in, the intent of your practice—those are the things that are going to generate where you're going to be. We look at genetics as the starting point for a player. People always say, "Well, it's all about genetics." But that's simply not true. Genetics is just where you start. What it's really about is what you do with what you have. When people pull out the genetics or freak theory, I always point to guys like Dustin Pedroia. Or Tim Lincecum, who is just a skinny, scrawny guy. He's a very small guy, but he's very powerful. And of course, I think the most powerful example of this idea is Michael Jordan. You know, people say, "Michael Jordan is the greatest basketball player on earth, and he was just a freak." But everybody has heard the story about MJ getting cut from his high school basketball team when he was 16, right? So was he a freak when he was 16, or was he just a normal guy back then? Did he just become a freak overnight when he went to college? The reality is that getting cut is probably the best thing ever to happen to Michael Jordan because it gave him a new meaning, a new focus, and a new goal, which was to work his butt off and get back on the team. He worked harder than everybody else.

To put it simply, how hard you work, the hours you put in, and the intent of your practice are far more important. I do not believe in the prodigy theory, and I do not believe in the freak theory. I do believe in the 10,000-Hour Rule.

8. Baseball-Specific Strength & Speed

This component is very important for older kids,

especially those who are getting ready for college or who are college age. If you want to become great at baseball, you have to train yourself for baseball.

We have seen players get into the weight room, put on more bulk, and get stronger—and then they start hitting with less power and throwing with less power. So they can get stronger, but it doesn't mean that they're "baseball strong." An offensive lineman, even though he's big and bulky, isn't going to throw a baseball 90 miles an hour. He isn't going to hit a baseball 100 miles an hour. So you have to develop strength that is specific to your sport. What I mean by that is that you have to consider two things—you have to have overall body strength from head to toe, you have to be physically fit, but you also have to have rotational strength.

So everything you're doing in terms of baseball has to involve building strength and having flexibility at the same time. Now, most people understand that they're either stronger or they're more flexible. And you're probably going to have to work on whichever one is your weaker point. So if you're a guy who is super-flexible but who doesn't have a lot of strength, you're going to have to spend more time on your strength. If, on the other hand, you're a guy who is pretty strong but you're really tight, you've got to start working on your flexibility. If you don't have the flexibility, it's very difficult to become a 100-mile-an-hour hitter.

The other thing to think about is that baseball is a short-duration, quick-burst exercise. Some coaches recommend what they call "running poles," which is running longer distances, as good training for baseball. But this type of exercise doesn't fire the same fast-twitch muscles as if you ran a sprint. So baseball players need to train in the ATP-CP energy system. That's the system that you build in the first 12 seconds of any exercise. You need to go as hard as you can, but for no more than 10 or 12 seconds, and then you give yourself a break. The reason for doing this is that in baseball, everything happens inside of that 12 seconds. It takes you about a second to swing a bat. It takes two or three seconds to pitch a ball. It takes you four to five seconds to run down to first base. If you're an infielder, and the ball is hit to one side or the other, the play is over inside of four or five seconds. So when you run long distances, you're actually using a secondary energy system that allows you to survive the length of the activity. But when you're training for baseball, you need to do things in a quick-twitch, fast-burst way—go hard and then stop. Running long distances isn't going to help. Simply put, if you train slow, you become slow.

9. Energy, speed, and variation

Let's start by talking about variation. Variation means that you don't want to do the same thing over and over again. Otherwise, your training gets stale and your body stops growing. And what I mean by that is that it stops being challenged. Variation, for example, could mean a hitter taking three to five swings with his normal bat. And then he takes another three to five swings with a bat that's slightly longer or heavier. After that, he would take another three to five swings with a bat that's slightly lighter. Maybe then, he would take three to five swings hitting a regular baseball, after which he takes three to five swings hitting a heavy softball, and then another three to five swings hitting a very light ball. The point is, you have to constantly change your environment to make things more difficult, but also to keep your training sharp. It challenges you, but at the same time, it keeps you from training in a stale environment.

Then you have energy. One thing I see when people work with hitters is that they don't look at energy. A hitter can have a pretty swing. He can have a really nice-looking swing, but the energy that's going through his system is still very important. So picture this—if I'm going to hit the ball 400 feet and hit it 100 miles an hour, does that take a lot of energy? Of course it does! A nice, easy, lazy swing isn't going to make a ball travel 400 feet for most people. So you have to use the energy that's in your system and really get after ways of creating energy. One of the reasons we measure bat speed is that we're trying to measure how much effort you're putting into the swing. Energy is very important when it comes to creating power.

For speed, that's the ATP energy system at work again. You've got to work fast in order to fire those fast-twitch muscles. Most guys have a tendency to work slow instead of fast. They have a tendency to work more on strength versus speed. What I'm finding instead is that most people need to focus on working fast more than working strong. An example of what I'm talking about would be to swing a lighter bat or a broomstick or something that allows the body to move faster. The reason for this comes from the body itself, which is designed to conserve energy. We just do that naturally. So getting the body to move fast is a challenge in and of itself. We've got to get in tune with doing fast-twitch training, which is getting the body to move quicker. And that's why it's so important to do all the measurements, because it's really measuring how fast you're moving.

Words from a Valued Client

Mike Ryan is a master teacher and motivator. When it comes to teaching how to become more athletic, explosive, and powerful at the plate, Mike is one of the very best. Uniquely, he has taken many of Texas Baseball Ranch's principle for throwing and incorporated them into hitting. He has also developed several proprietary techniques and drills of his very own. My son visited his facility in Chicago last summer. While there working the program for only four days, he increased both his bat speed and exit speed by 7 mph. It was undoubtedly the best hitting instruction that my son has ever experienced. If you are truly looking to become more dynamic at the plate, I could not more highly recommend Fastball USA.

Jack Sells
Sales Search America
President

Chapter Five - Technique

Batting stance

One of the first things that comes up whenever anyone talks about hitting is batting stance. But even an eight-year-old can tell you that batting stance isn't important. You name your top ten favorite players of all time, and I guarantee you that they all have a different batting stance. None of them stood exactly alike. What that tells you is that batting stance simply isn't important. What's important is what happens after you get into your stance.

If you have a coach who is trying to teach you how to stand, that's not a good thing. You need to focus on the things that are important, on the things that good hitters are doing alike, not on the things that they aren't doing alike. If someone puts an emphasis on batting stance, then that's usually an indicator that that person doesn't know what he's doing. You want to stay away from coaches who are trying to create a cookie-cutter approach to swinging in one way or another. I'm not even a big fan of the word "mechanics." Whose mechanics are we going to criticize, or for that matter, emulate? Albert Pujols' mechanics? Jose Bautista's mechanics? They're all so different that you can't really talk about one guy's mechanics over another.

The most over-coached part of hitting is the batting

stance. All big league hitters hit from a different stance. Simply experiment with different stances until you find one that works best for you. Even then, always be open to change if and when needed.

Kevin Youkilis hit something like this.

Cal Ripken Jr. hit like this at one point in his career. He called it "the violin."

All stances are different. Some start open with the front foot dropped back. Others will start with the feet level or straight. Some will start with the front foot closer to home plate than the back foot.

A Very Important Lesson if You Want to Hit Harder and Farther

Regardless of how hitters start, they will ALL get into nearly the exact same position when the front foot is landing as they complete their stride

Great hitters will look very different before they begin to stride. Great hitters will look almost identical when the stride foot comes down.

You can work hours and hours on your swing, but if you're NOT in the right place when the front foot lands, then the swing will not be very efficient.

Here is a demonstration of what a big-league hitter looks like after the stride:

Check Points:

- A. Feet are wider than shoulders.
- B. The back knee is NOT directly over the back foot. Instead, the knee is inside the back foot.
- C. Legs resemble a triangle.
- D. Front shoulder is lower than back shoulder.
- E. The bat head should appear in the imaginary

window above the head.

F. The middle of the bat should not be far off the back of the head.

G. The bat is angled back towards the pitcher.

H. Hands are behind the back shoulder with wrist cocked.

I. The front arm has some bend. The bend should be closer to an obtuse angle.

Most Common Mistakes

- Bat is NOT in the window and is too flat.
- Back knee is almost over the back foot.
- Feet are not wide enough.
- Front shoulder is higher than the back shoulder.

Movement versus position

Most coaches teach hitting by focusing on position. By this, I mean they have hitters practice like this: step one, take your stride; step two, turn your hips; step three, move your hands; step four, take your swing. The problem with this method is that practicing positions does not give you a feel of the energy that's involved in hitting a ball 400 feet.

Instead of positions, what we focus on is how hitters move in between those positions. Movement is so much more important than positions because, by definition, hitting is a movement. And you have to learn how to move like a Major League hitter, not how to stand like a Major League hitter. Once you learn how to move, you'll start to learn how to create more power and energy through the system.

One of the biggest hitting myths out there in terms of movement is something known as "squashing the bug," where coaches tell hitters that they need to turn and pivot on their back foot. There's no doubt that Major League hitters do not turn and pivot on their back foot. Most hitters, when they actually hit the ball, are only touching the ground with the tip of their shoe. The ball of the foot is off the ground, and, in a lot of cases, their back foot is off the ground when they actually hit the ball. If you have somebody trying to teach you to squash the bug, you need to run the other way! There's simply no bigger myth than squashing the bug. That is not what elite hitters do.

Another issue with movement, in terms of hands and the front arm and sequence, is that coaches try to teach hands to the ball, or hands inside the ball. What happens is, hitters are now being trained to get their hands moving first, which gets their hands in front of their hips. Most of us learned when we were kids that the hips should lead the hands, not hands before hips. But nowadays, we have so many coaches out there placing an overemphasis on teaching hands that it gets hitters out of sequence and it really forces the hitter to bend his front arm to a point where he's artificially swinging the bat. A hitter can't generate homerun power doing that because it's a very unnatural position.

Stay positive

So many times, you'll hear coaches and parents focusing on what kids are doing wrong, especially with hitting. What we really need to focus on is what kids are doing right. For example, a coach will say, "Don't swing at the high pitches." "Don't pull your head out." "Don't step out."

Instead of focusing on what not to do, focus on what they should be doing. Studies have shown that if you coach with negative comments like that, you're just more likely to reinforce the negative behavior. I like to say things like, "Keep your head still." "Step straight at the pitcher." Keep your comments positive and focused on what you want the hitter to do as opposed to what you don't want them to do. That's first. Be only a positive talker when you speak.

Batting tees

Coaches and hitters everywhere use batting tees, but what people have to remember is that batting tees are just a tool. Using a batting tee does not make you better as a hitter. The biggest mistake I see people making with hitters and batting tees that they get hitters too close to the batting tee. They stand with the tee almost as if the tee was home plate, and then they get really close to the tee because they want to practice an inside-out swing, where the hands come forward first. When you get that close to the tee, the hitter no longer has to use his body to hit the ball. So if a hitter is using the batting tee incorrectly, he's actually going to get worse as a hitter.

I would say this about using a batting tee. If you're going to use a batting tee, stay behind the batting tee and put the batting tee out in front of what would be home plate. That forces the hitter to have to move forward so he has to get his body involved in his swing. And then he's more likely to swing his hips before his hand, and he's also more likely to get good extension. Just don't put the hitter on top of the tee, or too close to the tee, or put the tee right over where home plate would be so the hitter doesn't have to move his body.

Three movements for better hitting

The building energy phase

At our academy, we find that hitting needs to be kept simple. So the first movement, the building energy phase, is really simple. It's loading while moving forward. We want to see that the hitter has some forward movement during his stride and, at the same time, we want to see that his front shoulder, his front hip, and his front knee are turning inward slightly as he's moving forward. Another way to describe this is as loading while moving forward. When we look at phase one, and we look at video of hitters in phase one, we definitely want to see that the hips have moved forward, and we want to see that the front knee, front hip, and front shoulder have turned in slightly toward the catcher while striding. That creates what we call a "rubber band effect" and builds more energy and more power into the swing.

In phase one, the front knee, hip, and shoulder stay turned inwards slightly as the body begins to move forward. Imagine that there is tubing attached to the front knee, hip, shoulder, and foot and that the umpire is pulling the tubing back as the hitter strides forward. The coiling up of the front while the body is moving forward creates a rubber band within the body.

45

Notice just as the foot is coming down that the front knee and foot are still turned inwards slightly. Also notice that the hitter is NOT sitting over the back leg. Instead, the back knee is inside the back foot and NOT directly over the back foot. The result is that the body is creating momentum forward, while the front half stays closed, creating torque throughout the body.

Notice the angle of the back leg as the stride is completed. This drives the weight to the inside part of the back foot, helping the hitter stay inside the ball. Most hitters who don't maximize power are still sitting over the back leg.

Also note how the front knee is still turned inwards, creating more tension and torque throughout the body. This hitter is a 6th-grader who has already hit a baseball 87 miles per hour.

Loading while moving forward creates maximum torque

Notice how the angle of the back leg changes during the stride, moving the hitter forward.

Notice how the front hip passes the cone, showing us that the hitter has transferred weight forward.

Once the front foot lands, forward momentum STOPS. The front leg locks out and often times the back foot will jump forward or up off the ground. The hips

49

and shoulders continue turning and rotating until the shoulders have replace each other. Notice where the hitter is in relation to the cone in the beginning compared to after the swing. Most hitters today are being taught NOT to move. This is a huge mistake. The body must move to the point at which the hitter is NOT sitting directly over his back leg.

Mastering the mid-turn

Next, we talk about mastering the mid-turn. The mid-turn is when the hips start to lead their way to the ball while the hands stay back. Remember, we talked earlier about the hips leading the hands. What happens is, during that hip turn when the hands stay back, you are able to create more power to the ball, and the wrists stay cocked. It creates what we call a "power-V" angle, which is the length of your lead arm all the way back up to the angle of your bat. And when you have a good mid-turn, it allows you, as long as your hands stay back, to hit breaking balls better, and it allows you to see the ball longer. That mid-turn is one of those things that all Major League hitters do alike. This is an area where all hitters need to focus. Remember, you want to copy what good hitters are doing alike, not what they do differently.

CREATING THE 100MPH HITTER

This picture shows the hitter during what I call the Mid Turn.

The hips and shoulders lead the way as the hands stay back as long as possible. Notice how the bat angles back towards his head and the bat head still appears higher than his head. The middle of the bat is even with the back of the head.

The key is having the front arm as long as possible and keeping the wrist on the front arm cocked. The hands should appear to be very close to the shoulders and there should not be much gap in between the bat handle and the shoulder.

The best hitters master the mid-turn movement.

Releasing energy into the swing
The third movement is this swing itself. What you want to see with a good swing is after contact, a hitter is going to see both arms get completely extended, and the bat head is going to point out at the pitcher with both arms fully extended. In my opinion, that is the result of a good mid-turn and a good swing. Once the hitter gets both arms extended, he wants the rotation to continue and the arms to stay extended as long as possible. The big mistake that we usually see hitters making in this phase is that they start to turn their hands and wrists over too early because they're trying to bring their hands back to their shoulder too quickly. I refer to that as "going home early."

The idea is to swing through and get full extension and then stay extended as the shoulders and hips rotate. This will give you much better ball flight and a lot fewer ground balls with your results.

Phase 3   Swing Through the Final Arch

Lower half, just before the foot plant

Notice the weight transferring to the inside part of the back foot. The knee is inside the back foot and the hitter is NOT squashing the bug.

The Mid Turn from the Side Angle

Hands Back
Good Bat Angle
Wrist Cocked

Weight is towards the inside part of the back foot - Not squashing the bug

The result is ...

At the point of contact, the front leg locks out and the back foot often releases forward. The front leg locking out helps create improved ball exit speed. If the front leg is too soft, the ball does not quite jump as hard or as far as it could.

The front leg locks out at and just after contact.

Half-Way Swing Point

The arms extend out to the pitcher and the right arm should be visible at maximum extension. I refer to this as the half-way swing point. If the right arm is not visible (for a lefty hitter), this would be a sign that the hitter has rolled his wrist over, which normally results in ground balls to the pull side.

Half-Way Swing Point – Extension

Three-Quarter Swing Point – Still Extended

Notice that the shoulders continued to rotate and the arms are still extended. The left arm has not yet rolled over the right arm, which is how you keep from hitting those weak ground balls.

In our Explosive Hitting DVD Video Series, we show you the FINAL ARCH drill sets that help you achieve greater ball flight by NOT rolling the hands and wrists over.

Rotation

When I tell a hitter he needs to finish his swing, I'm

really speaking about finishing the rotation. In my opinion, too many hitters are so worried about contact that they never finish rotating, which is half the reason they roll their wrists over and hit weak ground balls.

Rotation is power. You need to fully rotate. You need to rotate with tremendous speed. Baseball is a rotational sport. Hitting is rotation.

Who finishes big?

Think about it. Watch most hitters from outside of the United States and they finish big. This is how great powers hitters of the past also finished their swing. The problem is that we started coaching kids on how to be "pretty" with their swing. We started telling them to slow down, be controlled, be balanced, and most of all don't miss!

The Explosive Hitting System is designed to let hitters hit like they're having fun. The direct result is that those who train with this system hit harder and farther than everyone else.

Timing

Another really huge component of hitting is timing. Most of the time when we think about power hitting, we just think, "Explosive, explosive, explosive." But there's a little bit of calm in there too, and that's where the timing comes into it. We like to talk about it as "dancing with the pitcher."

To achieve good timing, the hitter needs to realize that everything he does is based on what the pitcher does. So, for example, you can't just swing when you want to swing. When you start your loading process—phase one of the three movements we just discussed, when you start to load and move forward—that's based on when the pitcher is starting to bring his arm forward. So, for example, if a pitcher is throwing a little harder than normal, you would start your movement a little earlier. This is the part where you're dancing with the pitcher. So you start your movement earlier if the pitcher is throwing harder. If the pitcher is throwing slower than normal, then you simply start your movement later. A lot of people think that if the pitcher is throwing harder, you need to swing faster, but that's not the case at all. Your swing needs to be the same speed and tempo every time. The main difference is when you get started.

Now, to simplify timing, we've come up with a concept we call, "Ready, go." It's just like when you're running a race, and you give the runners a "Ready, go!" Our hitters say this out loud when they're practicing, even if they're just practicing on a tee. When the hitter goes into his loading movement, when he starts to pick up his front foot and he starts to move, that's the "ready" part. We try to get them to practice syncing up their "ready" with the moment when the pitcher is coming forward with his arm. So the hitter gets ready early. Then, after the ball is thrown, that's his "go." When he swings, that's the "go." We get them to feel a sense of matching up their "ready, go" with the pitcher's own "ready, go."

I think one of the biggest mistakes a hitter can make is not to pay attention to the speed of the pitcher. Every hitter, even in the Major Leagues, is programmed to hit a certain speed. So a Major League hitter is programmed to hit about a 90-mile-an-hour fastball. When he sees somebody throwing 96 miles an hour, he is going to have to make a slight adjustment, and that slight adjustment is simply starting his "ready" movement earlier. If the pitcher is throwing a lot slower, then the "ready" needs to start a lot later.

Words from a Valued Client

In 20 months of intense training at Fastball USA, [my son] went from 73 mph to 97 mph bat exit speed.

His bat speed is also now 97 MPH which matches his exit speed! *To put this in its proper perspective, these numbers are the same as most major league ball players outweighing Dommo by 20 to 50 pounds.*

Dom Demicco

Chapter Six -
The Strategy Approach

There are three parts of the strategy approach to hitting that are important to remember: yes hitting, types of counts, and measuring success.

Yes hitting

"Yes hitting" is a concept that I started to understand and appreciate when I was actually playing baseball. I came to realize just how important this concept is. The opposite of a yes hitter is an "I don't know hitter."

Yes hitting is when the hitter has already determined, even before the ball has ever been pitched, that he's going to swing the bat. So he has predetermined that he's swinging. He's in what we call "yes mode." Yes mode is basically when the hitter goes, "Yes, yes, yes!" in his head. When the ball is pitched, if the pitch is a bad pitch, he simply needs to learn how to put on the brakes and then say "no." So even with a bad pitch, the hitter is saying, "Yes, yes, yes, no." It's a lot easier to stop than it is to go.

What I've found is that most hitters who are in slumps will come back and tell me that they were not in a "yes" hitting mode. Instead, they were in what we call an "I don't know" mode. In an I don't know mode, as the ball is coming out of the pitcher's hand, the hitter is unsure whether he's going to swing. He only decides after the ball is thrown whether he's going to swing or not going to swing. You will see on the field that hitters who are in an I don't know mode have a tendency to swing late. They also have a tendency to take good pitches that they later wish they had swung at, and they end up really, really struggling. One thing that's very important about yes hitting is that it's a great way to get out of a slump. If you go to the plate knowing that you're going to swing, all you have to do is learn how to stop. Learn how to not swing at bad pitches. In fact, that's how young kids should grow up hitting. They should be in yes hitting mode all the time. As they evolve and the more pitches they see, they simply need to learn over time how not to swing.

The problem is that we're living in a world where everybody wants to win now, so coaches are very concerned about drawing walks, for instance. So they're teaching hitters how to take pitches first and swing second. And that will actually eliminate power. When you react late to a pitch, you have to change your swing technique just to make contact. You will not have a normal, powerful swing if you take that approach.

Types of counts

Just like with everything else we do, we keep our philosophy about types of counts really, really simple. The way we look at it, there are only two types of counts. Either you have two strikes on you, or you don't have two strikes on you. It's that simple. When you have less than two strikes, you're in what we call a "double mode." In other words, it's double or nothing.

You're trying to be super-aggressive and get a pitch that you can drive and hit off the fence. You're super-aggressive in those counts. You're assuming fastball, and you're going to be very aggressive.

When you get to two strikes, that's the second type of count. Then we start to let the ball travel, and we really start to focus on hitting the ball to the opposite field and down to the other direction.

So, you either have less than two strikes, and you're being very aggressive, trying to hit the ball as hard and as far as possible, or you have two strikes on you, and then you're trying to expand the strike zone slightly and battle and really let the ball travel to a point where you can hit the ball hard the other way. The reason you want to focus on counts this way is that most pitchers who have two strikes on a hitter will throw the ball on the outer half of the plate or they'll throw a slower pitch. And by focusing on hitting the ball the other way, it trains you to let the ball get deeper and be more prepared for slower pitches and outside pitches.

Measuring success

We talked a little about this earlier, but it's worth repeating: Measuring success is a crucial part of your hitting strategy. The way you should measure your own success as a hitter is to keep a journal during the season and start tracking the percentage of hard-hit balls. When you do this, you will start to demand more of yourself as a hitter, and you'll start to understand that you're controlling the things you can control. Instead of tracking your batting average as, say, .250, track how many balls you hit hard during a game. So maybe you went 2-for-4 in a game, but only one of those hits was a hard-hit ball, so you would track that as 1-for-4. Track that percentage instead of tracking your batting average. Ultimately, that's what scouts are looking for—hitters who can hit the ball hard, even when they're making outs. I've seen a lot of people beat themselves up about not getting a hit when they're already hitting very well. And I've seen others not hitting very well, but they're still getting hits. They don't realize that they're already one or two steps into a slump and that they're not doing as well as they thought they were doing.

Words from a Valued Client

We have trained and played for Mike Ryan for two years now, and the improvement at Fastball USA is "hands down" better than any other place. My son has always had power, but things are much more refined (exit speed 96 mph) and he has more understanding behind the science of hitting a baseball.

Scott Svetic

Chapter Seven - Personalizing the Process

When a hitter personalizes the hitting process, he needs to look at two things. The first is to get really specific with the types of drills he needs. He should only be doing the drills that he is going to personally benefit from. My suggestion is to get a video analysis so he can start to personalize his drills. All of my online members around the country are given a process that is personalized to them.

The second part of personalizing the hitting process is a concept called "blending." I'm going to explain blending by first talking about anti-blending. Anti-blending would be if you hit off a tee for 15 minutes, then took short toss for 15 minutes, and then took batting practice for 15 minutes. That's an example of anti-blending. The reason this doesn't work is that whatever you worked down off the tee, you're not going to be able to remember or repeat 15 or 30 minutes later in batting practice.

Blending, on the other hand, would be, in this example, taking two or three swings off a tee, two or three swings in short toss, and then two or three swings of batting practice. Then you go back to the tee and repeat the process. Now you've created a connection between what you're working on off the tee, what you get out of short toss, and what you're doing in batting practice.

Most people will say that they're very good in the batting cage or they're very good off the tee, but they're not very good in a game. And part of the reason for that is that they don't blend what they're working on into what we call "game-like" conditions. So you want to make sure that, for whatever you're working on, you don't spend too long on it. I would recommend no more than three repetitions before moving on to the next thing that's closest to game-like. Then get into game-like conditions so you can see that your work is transferring over into the game itself as opposed to practicing 15 minutes of swings off a tee, then another 15 minutes of short toss, and then another 15 minutes of batting practice. That's not a good way to develop a great game swing.

Words from a Valued Client

"I had coached nearly 30 years without winning a high school state title. It is no coincidence that the year I implemented Mike Ryan's hitting methods our team won it all. Entering the year, our intent was to hit every ball hard. The only statistic we posted after games was Hard Hit %. That intense focus allowed us to double the number of extra base hits we had from the previous year. In the last four games of our championship run, we averaged 9.5 runs a game against the best pitching in the state. It's simple, if you want a lineup stacked with ferocious hitters then get with Coach Ryan's program."

Thanks again Mike,

Dave Savino, Glen Allen High School, Glen Allen, Virginia

Chapter Eight – Putting It Together with Coach Ryan

Now you know about why and how to become a 100mph hitter—the nine keys to training, the technique, the strategy, and personalizing your training. If you're ready to take it to the next level, there are a lot of ways I can help.

One way I work with young athletes is to do a personal mentorship program. I mentor fifteen to twenty baseball and softball players every year all around the country. It's an online program where I personally give them a video analysis and work with them remotely all through the year. Another way you can take advantage of my training is through our explosive hitting system DVDs. These DVDs include more than 20 drills and cover a lot of the techniques and processes that we do at our academy, Fastball USA, to develop a 100-mile-an-hour hitter.

If you're not in the Chicago area, in addition to the academy, we also hold boot camps. These are three-day camps that we typically hold during the school year. They run Friday night and all day Saturday and Sunday, so you can train with me for the whole weekend. We also do what we call road shows, where we bring the explosive hitting system to you. If you have a team or an organization that you want to experience the explosive hitting program, we'll set up an event and travel to you, so you don't have to come to us. I also do coach's clinics and seminars all over the country. I speak to coaches and organizations about how to implement the explosive hitting program into their systems.